mini ENCYCLOPEDIA

EARTH

Contents

D1114905

Earth from space

The Earth is just one of eight planets that circle around the star that is our Sun. The Sun and the planets together are called the Solar System.

Mercury

Venus

Earth

Mercury, Venus, Earth, and Mars are made up of rock and metal.

Mars

The Earth travels around the Sun once each year. This is what gives us different seasons.

Jupiter, Saturn, Uranus, and Neptune are made up of gases.

Jupiter

Saturn

Neptune

Uranus

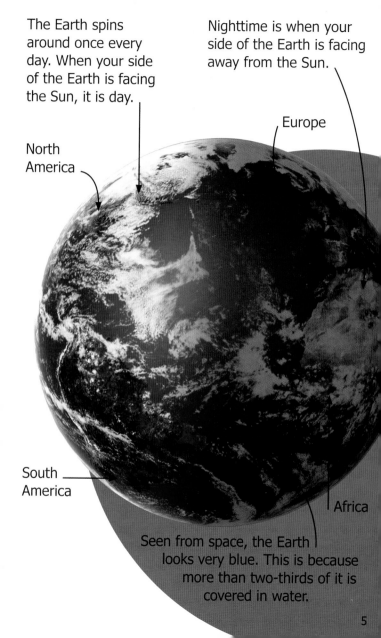

The Earth spins around once every day. When your side of the Earth is facing the Sun, it is day.

Nighttime is when your side of the Earth is facing away from the Sun.

North America

Europe

South America

Africa

Seen from space, the Earth looks very blue. This is because more than two-thirds of it is covered in water.

5

The Earth's layers

If you could cut through planet Earth, you would find a number of different layers. The crust on the outside is made of hard rock but is thinner than the skin of an apple when compared to the overall size of the Earth.

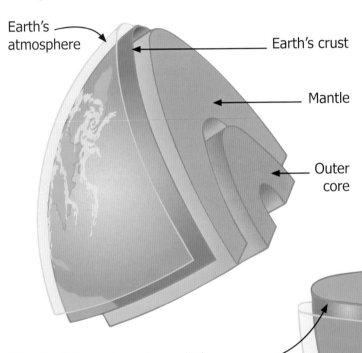

Earth's atmosphere

Earth's crust

Mantle

Outer core

The Earth's crust can be as little as 4 miles (6 km) thick under the oceans and as much as 44 miles (70 km) thick under the continents.

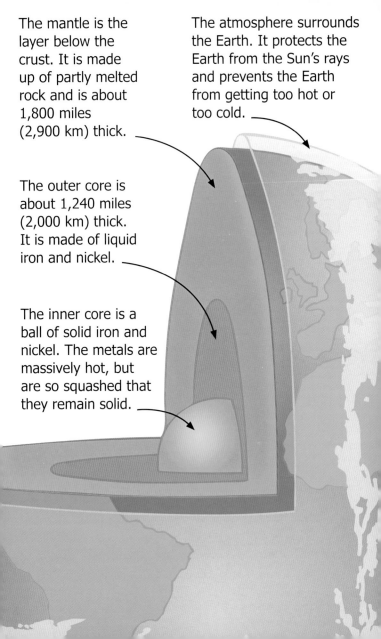

The mantle is the layer below the crust. It is made up of partly melted rock and is about 1,800 miles (2,900 km) thick.

The atmosphere surrounds the Earth. It protects the Earth from the Sun's rays and prevents the Earth from getting too hot or too cold.

The outer core is about 1,240 miles (2,000 km) thick. It is made of liquid iron and nickel.

The inner core is a ball of solid iron and nickel. The metals are massively hot, but are so squashed that they remain solid.

Moving continents

The Earth's crust is made up of huge sections of rock known as tectonic plates. These plates fit together like an enormous jigsaw puzzle. The Earth's plates are always on the move, because of the partly melted mantle underneath them.

South America

New rock ridge

When two plates move apart, molten magma pushes up to fill the space, forming a ridge of new rock.

Fold mountains

When plates push against each other, they can force the rocks up in folds, forming huge mountain ranges.

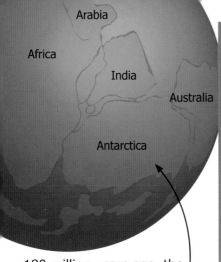

Arabia

Africa

India

Australia

Antarctica

180 million years ago, the continents looked like this. Since that time, the Earth's plates have moved and large areas of ocean now separate some of the continents.

Volcanoes

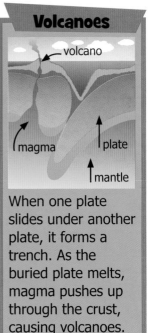

volcano

magma | plate

mantle

When one plate slides under another plate, it forms a trench. As the buried plate melts, magma pushes up through the crust, causing volcanoes.

Earthquakes

If one plate pushes sideways past another plate, it can cause earthquakes.

Finger fast

The Earth's plates move on average 1 in (2.5 cm) every year. That's about as much as your fingernails grow in the same time.

Volcanoes

A volcano erupts when red-hot molten magma rises up from deep within the Earth and forces its way out. The magma may spill out of a long crack, or erupt explosively, hurling rock, ash, and gas high into the sky.

The lava is so hot that it would melt steel.

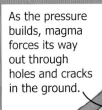

As the pressure builds, magma forces its way out through holes and cracks in the ground.

Clouds of ash and gas pour out of the crater – the hole at the top of the volcano.

branch pipe

main pipe

Each time the volcano explodes, another layer of lava or ash forms.

Molten rock, or magma, rises up the volcano's main pipe and up branch pipes.

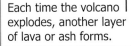

Volcano shapes

When lava is runny, it spreads out quickly and the volcano that forms is quite flat. When lava turns to ash, it forms a low volcano. When lava is thick and sticky, it does not spread easily and forms a volcano with a pointed cone.

Flat volcano

Low volcano

Pointed cone

Earthquakes

When the Earth's plates push against each other, the rock can suddenly slip. This causes an earthquake. The Richter scale measures how strong an earthquake is and how much damage it does. Every few months, a major earthquake takes place somewhere in the world.

Houses collapse.

Tsunami

An earthquake under the sea causes a huge wave, called a tsunami. The wave can be as much as 197 ft (60 m) high and creates chaos when it reaches land.

Broken gas pipes and electricity cables cause fires.

Telephone lines fall down.

Roads are destroyed.

Rocks and minerals

Igneous rocks form when molten magma in the Earth's crust cools and hardens. Sedimentary rocks form when layers of sand and mud build up and are crushed and dried. Metamorphic rocks form when sedimentary or igneous rocks are heated and squeezed.

The river carries tiny fragments of rock down to the sea.

Layers of sediment form on the seabed. After a very long time, they form sedimetary rocks.

Minerals

Minerals are the building blocks of rocks. If you look at a lump of granite, you can see its different minerals: biotite, quartz, and feldspar.

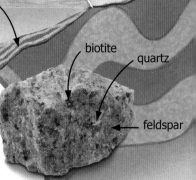

biotite

quartz

feldspar

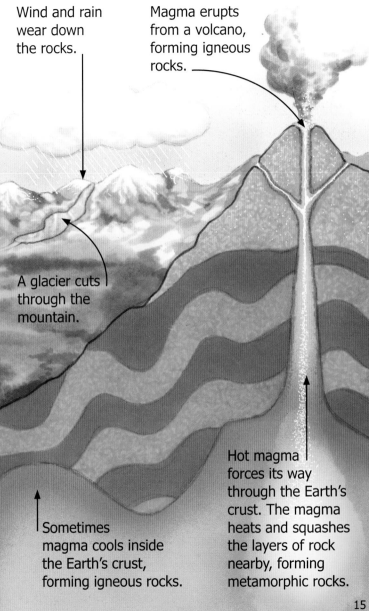

Wind and rain wear down the rocks.

Magma erupts from a volcano, forming igneous rocks.

A glacier cuts through the mountain.

Sometimes magma cools inside the Earth's crust, forming igneous rocks.

Hot magma forces its way through the Earth's crust. The magma heats and squashes the layers of rock nearby, forming metamorphic rocks.

Oceans

A view of the Earth from space shows just how much of it is covered in water. Seas and oceans make up more than 70% of the Earth's surface. Much of the ocean floor is flat, but there are also steep mountains, wide ridges of rock, and deep trenches.

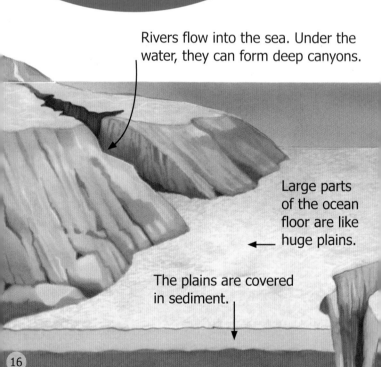

Rivers flow into the sea. Under the water, they can form deep canyons.

Large parts of the ocean floor are like huge plains.

The plains are covered in sediment.

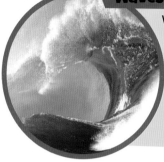

Winds blow over the surface of the sea and cause waves. The water in the waves travels in circles. When a wave reaches the shore, the circle is broken and the wave breaks on the beach.

Where one plate pushes under another, deep trenches form. These can be 6.2 miles (10 km) deep.

Volcanoes erupt from the floor of the ocean.

Long, wide ridges form where the Earth's plates move apart.

Molten rock wells up and forms new seabed.

17

Mountains

As the plates of the Earth's surface push against each other, they create towering mountain ranges. Gradually, over millions of years, these are worn down by wind, snow, ice, and water.

Fold mountains

When the layers of rock bend upward, or push on top of each other, they can form huge fold mountains. The Himalayas are fold mountains and are the highest mountains on Earth.

Fault-block mountains

If the layers of rock crack, a section can push up, forming a fault-block mountain.

Dome mountains

Sometimes magma in the Earth's crust forces the rock above it to move up, forming a dome mountain.

Volcanic mountains

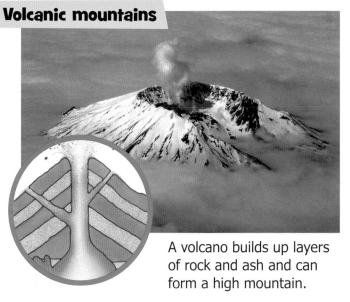

A volcano builds up layers of rock and ash and can form a high mountain.

19

Glaciers

Glaciers are huge rivers of ice that are heavy and strong. As they move very slowly downhill, they carve through rock and push it out of the way like a bulldozer.

Snow falling high on the mountains does not melt.

Streams flow under the ice of the glacier.

The end of the glacier is called the snout.

New snow presses down on the old snow, turning it to ice.

Glaciers only move a little over an inch each day.

The ice wears away the rock to its side and underneath it and carries rocks and stones along.

Ice float

When glaciers flow into the sea, blocks of ice break off and float away. The blocks are called icebergs. Only a small amount of the ice shows above the water level.

Rivers

Rivers are powerful forces, able to shape the land through which they flow. They wear down the rock in some places and build up new ground in others.

Streams join together to form a river.

As the river flows downhill, it wears away the rock to form a V-shaped valley.

The river flows quickly over steep, hard rock.

Where hard rock does not wear away, a waterfall forms.

Where the land is flatter, the water moves more slowly. The river bends, or meanders, from side to side.

Mighty Amazon

The Amazon River carries more water down to the sea than any other river in the world. It is also the world's longest river.

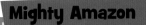

When the river reaches the sea, it deposits the sand and mud that it has been carrying. This builds up small islands, dividing the river into streams and forming a delta.

Deserts

One-fifth of the land on Earth is rough, dry land called desert. Some deserts are hot, others are cold, but all are very dry, with less than 10 in (25 cm) of rain each year.

The mountains of sand move across the desert, blown by the wind.

Did you know?

The Sahara desert covers more than 3.5 million square miles (9 million square km). It is the largest desert in the world.

Many deserts have huge sand dunes.

With no clouds in the sky, it is very hot during the day but really cold at night. The Sahara Desert can be as hot as 136°F (58°C).

Sand dunes can be as much as 100 ft (33 m) high.

Sahara Desert

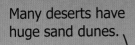
Gobi desert

The Gobi desert is a land of rock and gravel. It is very hot in summer but extremely cold in winter.

Coastlines

The coastline is the place where the land meets the sea. It is constantly changing shape, as waves wear away the land in some places and build it up in others.

When caves on both sides of the headland meet, a natural arch is formed.

Sandspit

Waves carry pebbles and sand from one part of the coast to another.

Sometimes waves deposit sand and mud in a long strip, called a spit.

If the top of the natural arch collapses, it leaves only a pillar of rock, called a stack.

Waves wear a hole, or cave, in the cliff.

Sand hills

When there is lots of sand on a shore, the wind sometimes blows the sand into mounds called sand dunes.

Climate

The overall pattern of weather in an area is what we call its climate. What the climate is like depends on how far north or south a place is, how high it is above sea level, and how close the ocean is.

Tropical
Mediterranean
Deserts
Mountains
Temperate
Polar

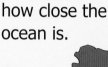

Tropical climates are hot with lots of rain all year round. Rain forests grow quickly providing a home for many animals.

The **mediterranean** climate has hot, dry summers and cool, wet winters.

In **polar** regions, the temperature does not get above freezing in winter.

A **temperate** climate has cool winters and warm summers. Lots of the plants and trees do not grow in the winter because it is too cold.

In the **mountains**, plants cannot grow on the rocky peaks, because it is too cold. Many plants and animals live on the lower hills.

In hot, dry **deserts**, very few plants or animals can survive.

29

Glossary

The glossary explains some of the harder words in this book.

atmosphere The blanket of gases that surrounds a planet.

climate The usual weather in an area.

continent One of the seven large areas of land on Earth.

desert A place where there is less than 10 in (25 cm) rain each year.

earthquake A sudden movement in the Earth's crust that causes violent shaking.

glacier A huge area of ice that moves slowly down a mountain.

iceberg A large block of ice floating in the sea.

igneous Rock formed when molten magma cools.

lava Magma that has burst out of a volcano and cooled.

magma Molten rock from inside the Earth.

mantle The layer that is below the Earth's crust.

metamorphic Rock formed by heating or crushing existing rock.

minerals The elements that make up rocks.

mountain A part of the Earth's surface that rises high above its surrounding area. Mountains often have steep sides.

planet A large, round object that travels around a star.

sedimentary Rock formed when layers of sand or mud are dried and crushed.

solar system Our Sun and the things that group around it, including the planets, moons, asteroids, and comets.

star A huge ball of burning gas that gives out heat and light.

tectonic plates The massive plates of rock that form the Earth's crust.

tsunami A huge wave of water that can occur when an earthquake takes place under the sea.

volcano The place where hot, liquid rock breaks through the Earth's crust.